Turkey

East meets West

Stephen Platt

www.leveretpublishing.com

Turkey: East meets West
First published - January 2013
Second Edition - September 2017
Published by
Leveret Publishing
56 Covent Garden, Cambridge, CB1 2HR, UK

ISBN 978-1-9124600-3-8

Turkey

East meets West

Turkey 2012

The route: Izmir – Van – Kars – Van – Ankara – Istanbul

İzmir

Tuesday, 18 September
After the steadiest of flights we arrive about 8 pm and wait for Bahar who had expected us to take longer getting our baggage. An hour's ride on the metro takes us to the family apartment where Bahar has prepared vegetables and rice with a cucumber and yogurt soup, ideal after a long journey.

Karşiyaka, the area where Bahar lives, is on the 'other side' or north shore of İzmir Bay. Her parents moved here 22 years ago from a big family house her grandfather built. A while ago they started to demolish old houses in İzmir and this transformation, from two storey self-built houses to apartment blocks, is happening all over the city. This was the widest street in the area when Bahar's father was working here and his boss, as well as teaching him the construction trade, helped him to buy the apartment. It's on the sixth floor overlooking a wide avenue. The train used to run down the middle but has been re-routed underground and what was once the railway track is now a pedestrian boulevard with trees and kiddies swings, lined with small local shops and cafes.

We are in Bahar's old room and Bahar is using her parents while they are at their summer home in Foça. We have to leave the window and blind open to get enough air, so are awakened at 6am by the call to prayer from the nearby minaret.

Wednesday 19 September
We make a slow start with breakfast at home on black tea, olives, feta cheese, tomato, cucumber, chives and simit-gevrek, a doughnut kind of local bread. Bahar sits cross-legged next to me on the sofa planning my itinary and telephoning people who might be able to help. She is gentle, calm, intelligent and efficient and contacts people in Van and arranges to see someone in the Disaster Management Centre here in İzmir tomorrow. She doesn't start teaching until next Monday so we have her company this week.

Last night we were talking about the family photos on the sideboard. There was a photo of her brother when he was about thirteen and Scharlie asked how old he was now. Quite calmly Bahar said he passed away when he was fourteen. "Sorry I didn't tell you," I said. "We were in a big car accident. My father was driving. He has never talked about it." Bahar was very close to her brother and his death has shaped her life. "It is still an issue", she said.

The TV news was filled with stories about Syrian refugees pouring over the border. Bahar commented "There are more each day and we can't feed them all. They are causing problems in the city centres where they are begging for food and shelter. The international community are not helping. Turkey is also having a resurgence of Kurdish nationalism. Erdoğan, the Prime Minister, promised to deal with demand for autonomy, but nothing has happened and people are getting frustrated."

We walk to the sea; it's only 10 minutes. The avenue is fragrant with the scent of lavender and jasmine, which covers the entrances to some apartments. We catch a bus along the front. It is crowded and as we stand in the centre where it 'bends' we get a sort of in-journey pilates session from the twisting platform.

The market is fabulous – mainly fruit and vegetable stalls and cheap children's and women's clothing. It is shaded by huge canvases and cooled by sea breezes; a friendly and colourful haven. Inexpensive clothes are piled on tables or hung in bright banners over the alleys between the stalls. But the food is the most colourful. The stalls are run by people who grow their own produce in the villages surrounding İzmir and bring them into town to sell. Housewives pulling canvas shopping trolleys compete over the piles of cheap coloured t-shirts or buy big plastic bags of green beans, tomatoes and aubergine. The variety of fruit and vegetables is astounding – peppers, olives and tomatoes of all shapes, sizes and colours. Herbs and wild plants are freshly picked and tied in loose bunches. We wander. Scharlie and Bahar are interested in the blouses. We browse in

Scharlie, Bostanlı market

Bahar in Bostanlı market

Crepe making, Bostanlı market

Spice stall, Bostanlı market

a haphazard, follow your nose kind of way and are attracted by a stall where women are rolling dough into wafer thin rounds, which are baked on a metal dome over a small brazier. They add cheese and spinach. The woman folds it and divides it into three and serves it to us wrapped in twists of paper and we amble on, happily munching. We try olives chosen from at least forty different varieties and settle on a mix of yellow and pink. Green walnuts are cracked for us to try. We taste cheese and buy two or three kinds. We buy samphire and one of the many kinds of spinach, tomatoes and brown bread.

We return home by taxi and lunch on our freshly bought produce. Drowsy from heat and travelling, Scharlie has a sleep until dark. She wakes about seven and puts on her lightweight blue cotton dress to go out for dinner. We take a taxi to a fish restaurant called Deniz on the edge of the bay, near the new development of high-rise apartments, called Mavişehir, that Işin studied for her PhD. There is a massive sports centre too where Bahar said she used to spend her weekends.

In her research Işin expected to find that social interaction was stronger in the old city where people can socialise but in fact she found that this expensive gated community was the most highly appreciated by residents because it felt safe and was prestigious. We prefer the neighbourhood where Bahar lives with people thronging the avenue in the evening and children playing out till late.

We sit outside, looking across the water to the winking lights on the other side of the bay. A crescent moon hangs low over the water and turns from yellow to dusky pink as we eat. The bream is very fresh and cooked whole.

On TV in England I watch cooking programmes and have been intimidated by how easily they bone fish, but it is so much easier to cook fish whole. Scharlie and Bahar choose red snapper and we finish the meal with a delicious pudding of semolina and ice-cream.

We walk home along the sea front, a route Bahar often runs. She says that a few years ago it was unpleasant as the smell from effluent was so strong. A new sewage plant has been constructed and a wide promenade has been built with landfill. Trees have been established and we pass small groups of people sitting out on the grass even though it's after ten. Originally the front was much further back and lined with private housing each with its own stretch of beach and private mooring. The rich moved away to high-rise apartments and the city planners proposed a dual carriageway along the sea-shore and began infilling. But the plans were opposed and the wide strip of reclaimed land is now a park to the benefit of the general populace.

We hear sounds of the Manchester United match in a café and go over to watch. Manchester is one up. Every seat is taken and patrons with camping chairs are sitting out in the pavement. A near miss by the Turkish team, Galatasaray, is met by a huge cheer. We stand watching until the action fades and move on to the next café, watching half an hour of the second-half in this erratic fashion. We are intrigued by the many street cats and dogs which all seem friendly and well fed. An old brown dog with a labrador body and dachshund legs ambles up expectant of a friendly rub of his silky head. Scharlie obliges and he follows us for a while. Bahar says volunteers feed and look after these strays and his metal ear tag means that he has been vaccinated against rabies.

Thursday 20 September

Today is my first day of interviewing – an engineer in the Disaster Management Centre in the Governor's Office in İzmir. The interviews were booked for 11.00 but Bahar rearranged it for 11.30 so we have time for breakfast on the top of a hillside called Seyirtepesi where Bahar's father suggested we go to get a view of the city and the bay.

Bahar's cousin Osman collects us in his car. He's gentle and quiet and has only a little English. The hillsides are dry and rocky with low growing aromatic bushes and pine trees. Scharlie asks if it is greener in spring, but Bahar seems to think it is too dry here but there might be new growth and spring flowers.

It was misty and the view poor. But we can see the city and get an idea of the north shore of the bay even if we can't see across. Gradually the haze clears during our leisurely breakfast – six different kinds of cheese, olives, tomato, jam and honey. A young man at the next table seems agitated and we realise why when our food arrives and wasps descend. The young man and his family move inside, but we just ignore the buzzing and get on with our breakfast. A wasp falls into the honey and its wings and body become so saturated that it sinks. Scharlie fishes it out with the tip of her knife and it hauls itself out to the lip of the dish. She places it gently on a clean plate. After a while it manages to clean itself and miraculously flies away. Imagine what it would be like to fall into a vat of honey! My cappuccino has such a mountain of froth that I have to swipe it off over the edge of the balcony before I can drink it. Then we move on to çay, the strong Turkish tea served in a glass. Turks drink it with sugar as it is strong and bitter without. The waiter brings smoking ground coffee in a bowl and the wasps clear.

When we leave and get into the car, Bahar slams her door on my fingers. I yell and have to wait while she fumbles to release the handle. But we drive up to the restaurant and she gets a bag of ice, which completely cures the bruising. I regret not having applied ice to my fingers when I fell off on Stanage.

Driving back to the city Bahar points out the cemetery where her brother is buried. "We can go there if you like, to see his place." We find the tomb is under pine trees on the edge of the cemetery high above the city. The marble tombs are raised above ground level in the shape of rectangular coffins with simple headstones. Her brother is buried next to her father's mother. His tomb is simple white marble with inlaid black stripes. Flowers grow on the top and Osman fetches water for both graves and carefully washes the marble tops and waters the plants. He gets a tape from the car to measure the boy's faded picture to get it replaced.

Mustafa, Bahar's father, had bought a double plot thinking his parents would lie here. Bahar said her mother would be buried above her brother and her father above his mother. "There is nowhere for me", she says as her eyes fill with tears. I put my arm round her. Scharlie tells her about her parents' grave in Coniston with a view of the Old Man and how she and her brother had planted wild flowers and bulbs.

Osman drives us to the ferry at Karşıyaka and we sit outside in the fresh air and cross to the south side. This is the heart of the old city. There is a stone tower in the centre of the square in front of the Governor's Palace and a tiny

Konak Meydanı (Square)

Disaster Management Centre, Izmir

round mosque with a minaret. There is a security entrance with x-ray, which we set off, but the guard lets us through without bother or asking to see our passports or bags. The palace is cool with high ceilings, marble floor and lots of light and air.

The man I've come to see, Necmettin Şahin, is the acting director of the centre. He has grey hair and glasses and a gentle manner. At first he is formal but gradually relaxes and tells me about planning for new housing after the 1995 earthquake in İzmir. His office overlooks the square and his desk is in the corner with the best view. We sit at his long meeting table. There are two or three other people at computers, and like other places we've been, people seem to be pretending to work. Maybe this is unfair; I don't really know what they are doing. Bahar is an intelligent and fluent interpreter and the interview goes well. As we are walking through the rooms on the way out a man offers us tea and we stop and chat about England.

To reach the Agora we walk through the streets around the bazaar. There are shoe shops displaying their multicoloured wares as vertical artworks; shops with the grey and black suits worn at young boys' circumcision ceremonies; party costume shops with the red or green traditional long beaded dresses and matching hats. There are clothes shops and cafes, spice shops and shops selling "evil eyes". The streets throng with locals looking for a bargain or grabbing food from the street stalls.

As we cross the main road from the Bazaar there is a braking and a woman's scream. A young woman has been hit by a car and her mother is crying for help.

Shoe shop, Kızlarağası Han Bazaar

Circumcision suits, Kemeraltı Bazaar

A policeman appears, a crowd forms, the driver, a woman in a headscarf, leaps out of her car. There is nothing we can do to help, so we walk on.

The hillside Agora is still being excavated and there is a team of archaeologists sifting through rubble. The catacombs of the library of the basilica have been excavated and we can walk under the vaunted roof. The basement is largely intact with barrel vaulted tunnels and an underground water course. We come to an area of stone ribs open to the sky and hear the wavering polyphonic call of prayer from different parts of the city, strangely beautiful.

At ground level reconstruction is in full swing, and they have been matching and re-erecting tumbled sections of columns. Slim long-legged cats slink over the marble pavements or loll in the shade. The site is surrounded with a wire

Agora of Izmir

Crypt of the Basilica

fence and a rather unattractive car park. Bahar says there is an awareness of the tourist potential of these ancient sites and the car park may be removed. So much of the city has been demolished in its turbulent past, by violence or earthquake or by redevelopment, but heritage is making a come-back.

Smyrna, the ancient name for İzmir has been an important port in the eastern Mediterranean for millennia. There was a great fire and massacre here in 1922 when the Turkish army entered the city and set fire to houses in the Armenian quarter. Over half the population of 400,000 had been Greek or Armenian Christians and İzmir was known as the infidel city by the Young Turks, a fiercely nationalist political group in Istanbul. The Greek army left the city by ship and the Turkish army arrived a day later. The commander of the Turkish First Army was rabidly anti-Greek and did nothing to check his troops. Within four days fire started and, fanned by the strong breeze, it raged through the old city around this area, known as Pagos. Armenian men were chased and beaten to death, and the young women and children kidnapped. There are many contemporary accounts, the most authoritative written by American women teachers who write about seeing Turkish officers ordering troops to pour petrol into the houses and down the roads. The Greek and Armenian population fled to the harbour where they were kept for two weeks and systematically robbed and abused until ships arrived to evacuate them. Warships, including two British battleships, were ordered by their governments not to intervene. I asked Bahar about the fire and she gave us an alternative view that it was thought to have been started by Armenians in a scorched earth policy to leave nothing for the Turkish victors.

This is the popular story of the genocide in Anatolia. During WWI there were reports of mass exiles of Armenians into the Syrian desert and over a million people were said to have died. But this history is not taught in schools and would be denied by most Turks.

We had planned to climb the hill behind the Agora to the castle. The neighbourhood here was developed informally and is quite different from the planned city. But it was hot and we felt we didn't have enough time.

We walked back from the Agora through the main bazaar. The streets are lined with shops and roofed with taut cloth to give shade, the bazaar is a maze of alleys, many roofed, with internal courtyards where trees and pergolas give shade. Scharlie is attracted by the cotton towels for sale in one of the shops. The owner is good at talking up the evident quality of his wares. I pace around

Kizlaragasi Han Bazaar

Dinner with Gülden and Isin,

resisting offers of tea to the evident disapproval of the shopkeepers.

In the main shopping street we meet Gulden and Işin seated at an outdoor café. We order lentil soup followed by kebabs, meatballs and pancakes with cheese and spinach. There is no beer, so we walk down to the front to find a bar and watch the sunset.

Gulden says she had applied for a short-term scientific mission from the EU programme that's supposed to be funding my trip to spend two or three weeks at LSE. Unfortunately she was refused. Hopefully, there will be more money if she applies again. She asks who I am planning to interview and I show her my list. She said Murat Balamir had been her supervisor. We chat about what it is like to live in İzmir and get the impression she finds it parochial. Gulden asks me in what city I would most like to have lived. I say Cambridge is good. I like other cities like Barcelona and Rome but wouldn't like to live there. She says she loves London, and Bahar and Işinşin nod in agreement.

We are too late for the sunset, but we find a nice table by the side of the pavement overlooking the sea. There are shawls if you feel chilly. I ask for Efes – a draught beer that they serve in bottles with twists of lemon. Ugur Bozkurt, a planner who Bahar wants me to meet, turns up. His PhD is on earthquake recovery, so he is a good contact. But he has been doing his doctorate for seven years and has had to go back to work in the planning department. I think he must have got lost doing it. I take his details and will e-mail him, as we don't manage to talk about disasters because we get sidetracked into the Kurdish question. I wax lyrical about the IRA and the only solution being regional autonomy. Ugur is not convinced.; "Turkish identity is too important to sacrifice". Gulden has to leave. She has a six year-old and has been away in Istanbul and needs to be with him.

The ferry is chilly and so we sit inside and I doze. Winter is coming. The ferries are a relaxing way to end the day, but must be frustrating if you have to get to work. When Bahar was doing her Masters the journey she had to make to her university by ferry and bus along the north shore took an hour and a half each way. Her new university is closer but still across the bay. She is thinking of trying to find a flat or a room over there but is worried about upsetting her parents.

Friday 21 September

Today we plan to go to Ephesus. Işinşin has decided to take a day off and come with us. She has just started driving and is nervous and wanted to know if we preferred to go by bus but we choose to go with her in the car. This time we catch a ferry further up the coast, nearer to where she lives, and stand in the prow and feel the wind in our hair.

We cross the motorway. "I want to tell you something, this is where my brother died", Bahar says without preamble. "I was lying on the back seat and my father was driving. He was het up from some argument and had been drinking. My brother was standing and I remember him shouting, faster daddy, faster. My mother was asleep. She usually stopped him going too fast. My father lost control on the bend where the motorway from the hills reaches the coast. There was a loud noise and the car rolled over. My brother was thrown through the windscreen. My parents were badly injured and unconscious. I was relatively all right having rolled into the well behind the front seats. The police arrived and took me and my brother to hospital. I was shouting, faster, faster, my brother is dying."

"In hospital I was separated from my parents. We knew my brother was hurt but were not told until after he'd passed away. A doctor said, your son is not very well, you must be prepared. But he'd already died; he had suffered a haematoma and they hadn't been able to save him."

In time, life gained some normality and Bahar concentrated on her studies but neither she or her parents talked about it. Her father had gone into himself. He was alternatively angry and in despair – arguing and going out every evening to drink. Her parents had tried for another child but her mother miscarried. Gradually they came out of their grief. A friend suggested Bahar see a therapist. "That was the beginning of understanding, she said." The family are close but Bahar feels the weight of their expectations. She had to be the strong one after the accident and pretend she was fine, but she'd lost her brother, as well. She loves them very much but needs her independence.

Işin rang to say she had problems with the steering. We found a café in the petrol station and waited. She arrived after half an hour. Her neighbour had helped her take her car to a garage where they fixed it with a squirt of WD40.

We set off. Her clutch control still needs practice and she's nervous of overtaking, but she drives slowing and safely. We arrive in Ephesus and stroll across the car park. A parked car suddenly reverses furiously without the driver checking his mirror and is about to run into Bahar and Scharlie. I jump forward and slap my palm on his rear window and he brakes. Bahar and Scharlie leap away. He's furious that we yelled and banged on his car. Bahar says he would have run us over. He's unrepentant, blustering rather than admitting his fault. I give him the look, point to my eyes and then at his chest. He shuts up and climbs back in his car.

After a delay, while Scharlie checks out the postcards and a dress shop, we set off to explore the ruins. It's a wondrous place, approached along an avenue of pines, the wind sounding through the needles like falling water. We reach the paved road that leads from what was once the port to the amphitheatre. This must have been lined with shops and commerce. The amphitheatre is huge and has been restored a number of times in the past. There is still restoration

Harbour road, Ephesus

Amphitheatre, Ephesus

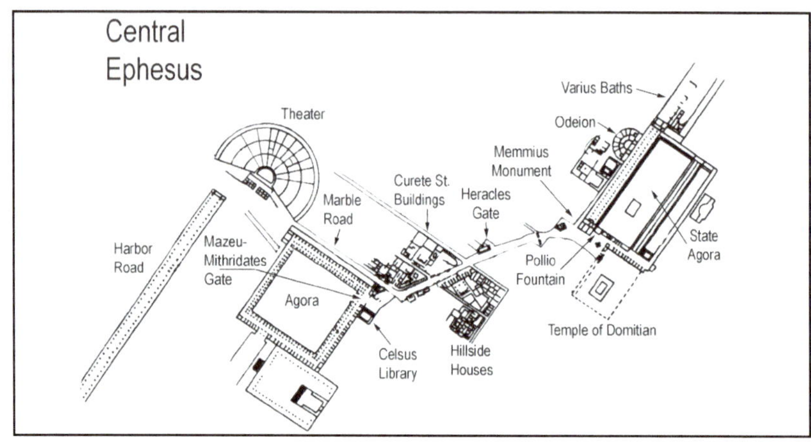

in progress. We sit on the steps in the sun soaking up the atmosphere and snapping pictures of each other. From here we take what must have been the main street of the town, past the house of pleasure and the public latrines and various temples.

A group of houses rising up on terraces have been excavated and opened to the public. They are under a huge aluminium tent like structure and you pay an extra 15 Turkish Lira (TRY) to see them. Işin encourages us by saying they have mosaics. They are well worth it. There is a glass walkway running round the whole complex so you can walk safely and not damage the archaeology. Three men are sorting bits of mosaic in a half-hearted manner. We pass different plunge pools and come to a huge half domed audience hall where the principal owner received guests. Although many of the treasures have been carted off

Celsus Library, Ephesus

Public latrines, Ephesus

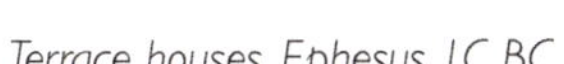
Terrace houses, Ephesus 1C BC

Terrace houses, Ephesus

to museums, there are mosaic floors, marble wall facings and wall paintings to see. Austria is paying for the restoration and roof.

As we climb the complex the apartments get smaller but no less comfortable. All the rooms have underfloor heating, there is piped water, pipes for sewage and each home is arranged around a communal courtyard or peristyle. The exit is at the top of the site and flagged walkways step down the hillside on either side of the block. The Roman Ephesians must have been fit since it is quite a climb. This wasn't the only apartment block but it is the best excavated and preserved. This must have been a big thriving city in antiquity.

We rejoin Bahar and Işin and continue our wander. The sky is blue, the pomegranates are ripe on the tress and we feel relaxed and unhurried. The top end of town is less excavated than lower down and we reach another entrance with a café and stop for tea while Scharlie buys postcards. We take the top road back past a small amphitheatre and various temples. The agora was also up here on the large flat area in the centre of the town. It is difficult to gauge how far it all extended but it is enclosed by steep rocky hillsides on two sides. Back at the entrance I wait, playing Sudoku on my IPhone while Scharlie spends half an hour with Işin and Bahar in the clothes shop.

It's a lovely evening; the sun is soft and golden and Bahar spots a road-side café hidden in trees and we sit on armchairs in the evening sunshine and eat fine lamb kebabs with cheese and spinach pancakes and ayran, a yogurt drink. The waiter, a wrinkled old man, is polite and sincere. He says it doesn't matter how small the meal is, as long as it is fresh.

Road side cafe

Bahar and Isin

Işin and Bahar are close friends and they each want the other to be happy. Işin has to decide whether to go to Prague to be with her boyfriend Vojtech but Bahar is not sure if he is right for her. Bahar is in love with Neil, a man she met in London, but her parents want her to marry a Turk and settle in İzmir and have a family. She doesn't know how it will work out with Neil, but is happy for the first time.

I sleep most of the way back in the car and doze on the ferry then pack quickly and head off for the metro to catch the 10 pm train to Foça.

Foça is a fishing village with a ruined castle in the harbour and ancient windmills on the hill above the town. We walk through the cobbled streets and have an ice cream on the harbour front – it was delicious, perhaps even better than Luca's gelatteria in Rome. Mustafa, Bahar's father, meets us on the front and drives us to their home on the outskirts of the town. Foça is a popular place for local people from İzmir and Bahar's parents camped here for years before they bought their house.

They are full of warmth and welcome and serve us a light meal on their terrace. They obviously adore Bahar and must have missed her a great deal when she was in England. They enjoy their life in Foça, spending the whole summer here, her father driving into İzmir to work most days. They have their own boat and love fishing. Nurşen, Bahar's mother, is a great cook and delighted to serve us her own home-made tomato paste and fresh home grown vegetables.

We meet their adopted dog Berduş, which means 'dead-beat'. His owner

Leaving Ephesus

Bahar's house and Berduş, Foça

runs the pension and is a lazy drunkard and Berduş spends his time sleeping in front of their house on the pavement. He is sixteen. There are also a couple of street cats.

Saturday 22 September

We rise at eight and Bahar invites me to swim but I get tea for Scharlie. Breakfast is an elaborate leisurely affair with cheese, olives, tomatoes, etc but with home made tomato paste, jam and honey on the comb.

We have decided to go to Pergamon today. It's about 40 km to the north of Foça and Bahar's mother has lent us her car. The drive along the cost is spectacular with lots of beautiful bays. Maybe Bahar is a little nervous driving because, although she knows we'd like to stop and take a photo, she can't find a place to pull in. We ask the way in the town below Pergamon and drive up to the cable car station but Bahar decides to drive. It's very steep, narrow and cobbled at first but then widens. At the top we find a tree to park under and Bahar gets out a picnic of vine leaf wrapped fingers of rice her mother has made for us.

Pergamon is an acropolis or hill fortress dominating the surrounding countryside and home to kings. Like Ephesus, it has been partly restored – this time by Germans who have been excavating here since 1878. Enough has been erected to give a haunting impression of the grandeur of the place.

There is a temple and amphitheatre where the rake of the seats is much

Sanctuary of Athena, Pergamon

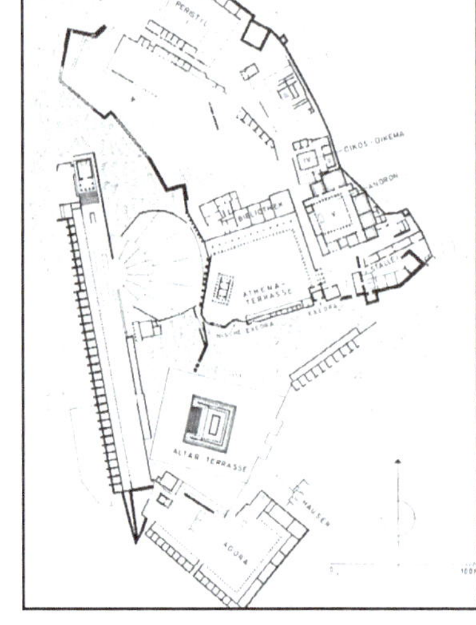

Map Pergamon

steeper than in Ephesus and gives a sense of vertigo. The guide says it seats 10,000 but I can't believe it until I count the rows and work it out in my head. We are all in a good mood and wander about in the sunshine. Sitting on a rock overlooking the reservoir, we chat briefly to a couple from California who are visiting the main biblical sites in Turkey. The afternoon draws on and we decide its time to leave. We miss the turn back to the coast road, the signs aren't clear, and have to take the road inland and Scharlie is disappointed not to get a photo.

Theatre, Pergamon

heatre, Pergamon

Bahar talks about her feelings for Neil and her parents' reaction when he visited her. They were very distant and made him feel unwelcome. We said it was only natural, especially because of the language barrier. But what a contrast to the behaviour with us. She said she didn't want to hurt them but she had her own life. The university was messing her about with a part-time contract with no holiday pay but the same amount of work. The highly respected dean had left and when Bahar had asked her why, she said the university was very disorganised. Bahar had also failed her TOEFL test. She'd got 92 out of 120 before she went to Nottingham five years ago. The university had demanded she retest and get 102 or more since this was a bureaucratic requirement. The only way she could do the exam was to go to Ankara and do the four-hour exam at test centre. She was tired and distracted and couldn't concentrate during the comprehension part and only got 89. The university said it was not urgent. So she's pissed off with them. Rather than look for a flat on the south side of the city, which will upset her parents any way, she's thinking of going to Istanbul and telling them it is better for her career. But her real dilemma is about Neil. Obviously her parents want her to marry a local and can't see why she makes life hard for herself. Neil is 47, is a musician, has a band and writes his own music. He also works in Sardinia as an adventure holiday guide. He liked Foça but would find life in Turkey difficult and Bahar couldn't stay in England without a job and work permit. She said she should have started looking for a job earlier but left it till the last 6 months. I asked her if she wanted a family and she said she was very negative about the thought of having children and she wasn't sure Neil wanted to settle down. She's seeing him this weekend

Sea front in Foça

Sun set Foça

Dinner in Foça

Harbour lights, Foça

in Istanbul and hopes to talk then. She said she meant to when he came last week but they had just had a quiet time together and she didn't want to spoil it.

We shower and change quickly and drive into town for dinner where we wander along the front of the curving bay, past the castle and stop for a glass of wine. Bahar, Scharlie and I walk back 100 metres to where we can see the sunset. It's chilly once the sun has gone down and I'm glad of the sweater I've been lent from Bahar's undergraduate days.

The owner and waiters are friendly because the family always go to the same restaurant on the front. We are invited to choose our fish, which look as if they were caught this morning. With Mustafa's advice we order.

There is a wedding party in the restaurant and they are serenaded by a couple of musicians with clarinet and drum. The bride and groom are past the flush of youth. He is podgy with a black moustache and bald head. She is buxom tall and well padded. But they are blissfully happy. She is in white and smiling shyly. He is bashful and a little dazed. They are sweet.

Our fish arrives and it's delicious, served with salad and yogurt and fine white wine. Bahar is fantastic at translating and keeping the conversation going. It's dark now and the many lights create coloured patterns in the water. The couple leave, walking away arm in arm. We in our turn are serenaded then wander back along the front to the car.

Sunday 23 September
We go swimming. It is not really cold but it's still not eas to dive in. The shore has big pebbles and it's hard to wade out. We swim out to Mustafa's boat and I climb aboard and sit in the warm early sun, while Bahar does lengths out to a large yacht. We sit in the sun for a while before returning for breakfast.

While waiting to go into town I take a stroll around the village with another dog that has befriended the Durmaz. It's friendly and wants to go for a walk. When we reach the main road it runs across. I decide not to call it back but a few moments later I hear honking and the sound of brakes and realise it must have crossed again. I've never seen such tolerance for street dogs and cats anywhere else I have been.

We are planning to go on a boat trip after lunch but first we go shopping. Scharlie wants to buy a pair of the baggy trousers like the ones Bahar wears and I want a Turkish mobile phone for my trip to Van. We find a nice looking shop and I walk along the main pedestrian street where I see a man's shop selling shirts and am taken by one in the window. So once Scharlie and Bahar have finished their trying on session, and Scharlie has found a skirt she likes, they accompany me. The salesman is friendly and I try on the shirt although there is no changing room and I have to strip off in front of everyone. He is a good salesman and persuades me to buy a second shirt because it matches my eyes. It has elbow patches I am not sure about. The cotton here is fine and much better and cheaper than in England. In a side street we buy a cheap second hand Nokia. With the sim it costs about £30.

Boat trip around Orak Adasi

Swimming at Hanedan beach resort

We had been hoping to set off on the boat straight after lunch, but Bahar's father's sister and family have arrived. Lunchtime lengthens and Bahar suggests Scharlie and I go to the sea and wait. Finally the family turn up, Mustafa carrying a jerry can of gasoline. To get out to the boat they have a pedalo that takes three – two pedal and one sits amidships.

We head out to sea. They want to show us the famous seals of Foça. But there are none to be seen, which doesn't seem to surprise anyone. We are out of the shelter of the bay and it's exhilarating. We are all sitting on the fore deck while Mustafa steers. Scharlie, Bahar and her mum are leaning against the cabin and I'm sitting on the prow. A larger wave threatens to bounce me off into the sea so I hold the rails to Mustafa's amusement.

We pull into a bay with a collection of modern looking white houses set in landscaped trees up the hillside. Bahar says it was a French holiday camp and that the government didn't renew their lease and it's been empty five years. She really likes the modernist architecture. We land and hop off into the water and wade ashore. The sand here is finer that in their home bay and I set off to explore. The complex is well laid out with each house having privacy and a good view of the sea. Scharlie dozes for a minute on the thick bed of dried seaweed with her back against the low retaining wall then we climb aboard and Nurşen takes the wheel and drives back on the sheltered side of the island.

They are putting things away for the winter, and this involves dragging the pedalo up onto the beach and locking her to the others. We don't understand why they are bothering if they come down most weekends since we're finding it very warm still. Nurşen has prepared lots of food in anticipation of our visit and we have something to eat back at the house. Then is able to use her mother's car to drive us back to since it's the end of summer and her mother will move back into town and needs the car there. For some reason I ask Bahar to check she has the flat key. The apartment door has two locks and is 2" thick with hardened steel bolts. I doze on the way and we are back in a trice. My premonition was right; Bahar can't make the key turn in one of the locks. I try and also fail.

We find a café and order a hot chocolate while Bahar tries with the neighbour and then rings her cousin Osman, who works for her father. He can't open it either so calls the locksmith who breaks the lock with his picks and we're in. I pack and go straight to bed. I had thought that my flight was early but I check and find it's not till two o'clock, which is great.

Van

Monday 24 September

Bahar leaves early for work We spend the morning at home catching up and then Nurşen and Scharlie walk me to the tube. It's an easy journey to the airport but much longer than I remember on the way in. Everything in the airport is straightforward and easy. I'm allowed my case and satchel and settle into a window seat and, after we gain altitude, watch Anatolia roll past with its folded grass hills and saltpan lakes. Suddenly, sooner than expected, we are over Lake Van and on our landing approach.

I get a taxi to the hotel which is out of town south of the airport. The hotel is luxurious, but I remember Bahar saying she got a good deal. I unpack, shower, telephone Scharlie, sort out my Internet connection, and do my email and its time for dinner. The dining room is on the ground floor and the smiling waiter takes my order. He likes me to order in Turkish because it amuses him and I order a salad and kebab with Rakı to drink. Rakı is the local spirit and turns cloudy when mixed with water and has a strong aniseed taste. I do some work and watch part of a film and get to bed.

Toki housing on landing approach

Rescate Hotel, Van

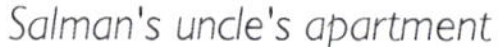

Salman's uncle's apartment

Salman's children

Tuesday 25 September

Bahar had found two possible guides for me and I had telephoned them both. One sounded competent but lacked a car and charged 300 TRY a day, the other sounded garrulous but had a car and charged 250 TRY plus petrol. So I'd contracted him.

He pitches up in the lobby at 8.30 as agreed but the vehicle turns out to be a clapped out green minibus with no seatbelts. "Not necessary", Salman beams, when I tried to find mine. Sitting high up in front of the windscreen I brace myself as he weaves around traffic into town.

I had persuaded Salman to drive to Erciş , the town nearest to the epicentre of the earthquake. He hadn't really wanted to go so far; it's 100 km each way. But before we set off he shows me his uncle's apartment block that is being demolished. "when there is hardly anything wrong with it", and invites me to see his hotel. He shows me the rooms and said I'd be much better off there than stuck in the expensive Rescate. Then he takes me to see his own house round the corner. It's a large house with a parking area and behind it there are other houses where his father and mother and various brothers live. There is a garden that his mother tends. I meet his wife, a diminutive shy woman in a headscarf, and his two children – a little boy of 6 and a girl of 3. I am served tea in their living room on their best couch.

Finally we set off for Erciş . We leave the ugly city and enter the lakeside country. Although it's autumn, and everything parched, there are still patches of green and some trees to relieve the barren hills and rock. I'm beginning to

Damaged mosque, Ercis

Main street commerce, Ercis

realise everything is in progress in this eastern province, not just the city that is being rebuilt, but the very landscape seems to have been but recently formed.

Erciş is a mess – even worse than the disorder and dirt of Van. Salman asks if I'd like to speak to the Governor and I say, " why not". The Governor is busy but will see us in an hour, so we take a walk through the town, such as it is. Although it's ugly, it is heaving with life and vitality. People are thronging about and the shops are selling all manner of foodstuffs and articles of everyday life.

Salman shows me the mosque, which has been closed and, as with every building he points out, asks me to pronounce on it's structural integrity and whether it should be demolished or repaired.

The mosque, he claims, is fine, pointing to where render has been chipped away exposing columns to check if they're cracked. Around the corner what looks like a department store is being repaired. All the columns have been encased in heavy-gauge steel reinforcing bar. Sheer walls are being created between the ground floor columns. The floor slabs have been broken around each column so that the new reinforcement can go down to the basement and up through each floor. Salman asks me what I think about the work and I say that I'm impressed with the quality but I am worried that the ramps that wind between the floors aren't properly tied into the columns. But what do I know. The owner, a distinguished elderly man with a moustache, introduces himself and I commiserate with him about his loss. He says the repair will cost £200,000 but demolition and rebuilding would be nearly twice as much. I give him my card and we shake hands.

Baroros Baran, District Governor Ercis

Death trap repair, Ercis

It's time to go back to the Governor who sees us after a short wait. He's young, in his thirties, and was sent to Erciş a month after the quake. He seems competent and intelligent and answers my questions politely and openly. He offers to read my report and help correct any errors. He spent some time in England and can understand and speak a little English although prefers to use Salman to interpret.

Outside we examine a building in a street next to the Governor's palace. Every column has sheered at the base and moved out of line, some by as much as 8". The exposed steel has bent or sheered. But Salman says they will patch it and people will forget. "They're making a virgin", he says. There will be shops below and apartments above. "It's a disgrace". he says. "Families with children will be killed". A man comes over to talk to us and it turns out he's also upset, but says that someone important and rich owns it.

We go back to the car and on the way pass what looks like a nice restaurant and I suggest we have lunch. The manager takes me upstairs to see what's on offer and I order green bean stew and rice. Salman orders meat. He says he has meat for breakfast, lunch, and dinner and can't do without it. My meal is good and I eat the salad without worrying that I'll get ill.

Wednesday 26 September

We drive back to Van and park near Salman's hotel again. Parking is chaotic here. People double-park, blocking one of the traffic lanes, or park badly and stick out. The pavements are broken where they are laying new services. They're installing natural gas, which should dramatically improve the city atmosphere as many homes still burn coal and wood.

We walk to his father's building. It's a standard concrete frame building with black basalt blocks filling the walls and old faded wooden windows. Salman asks me whether they should pull it down or repair it. I know the answer – "repair". The real question is when: now with an interest-free loan or later when Salman has made his imagined killing on the stock market. Only the ground floor is occupied with a variety of cheap looking shops. The one on the corner is his older brother's – a sad looking portly man with a moustache. They sell material for bedspreads and making clothes – probable the baggy trousers the women wear in the country. There are bolts of coloured cloth, a desk and a couple of chairs and a prayer board which the brother, a much more devout man than Salman, uses at least twice while I'm around. They have some business that involves exchanging wads of money. Apparently one of his sisters has just died of cancer and his niece needs to go and live in Istanbul. So the family has decided to buy a house there. Everyone has divvied up, but one brother seems not to have paid his share and Salman, the fixer in the family, has been tasked with finding the missing £8,000. He's borrowed it from a friend on a 10-day loan. And this is what the money exchange is about and involves each counting the notes ostentatiously but quite methodically. When we are in the car driving to the hotel Salman tells me that he's lost a lot in stock market trading. He explains in detail, but I can't follow. "It's why I have this sore on my mouth", he says, pointing, "with the stress".

Few traditional buildings survive

Classic döner kebab shop

There's something touching about this mountebank tilting against fortune. "I don't worry about dying", he says, "when it's your time, it's your time". I laugh. "Our Christian God expects us to take reasonable precautions", I say pointing to the missing seat belt. "Yes" he says. "In Islam we have to do what we can and then it's God's will."

I've adopted the pose of a good, or moderately good Christian, with Salman. One of his gambits with tourists is religion and he likes to take the moral high ground with decadent western atheists. So I trump him with Christianity and dredge my memory for my Sunday school bible teaching. His other favourite topic is women and love. Again he has an impression of the west from the Turkish media and the tourists he's met, that we are all fornicating drunkards. I say the media exaggerate. "Were you a virgin when you married", he challenges with a look of triumph? "Yes" I admit. He's flabbergasted. "I don't believe you", he says. "It's true, I was married at nineteen." "That's normal here" he says. "But divorce is common in your country", he suggests with what may be a tinge of envy. "I don't know what the percentage is but most of my friends are happily married and all our children have good stable family lives." I reply. He's amazed. "I've never met a tourist like you", he claims. I feel a little ashamed for painting a too rosy a picture. "We're all sinners," I say. "Yes", he admits. "It's difficult for me because I'm so attractive to women." I wonder if he means attracted. "When I take tourists we have to sleep in the same room sometimes. It's like petrol and a match – there is always fire. But I don't drink alcohol. I met two Slovakian girls when I was young. They were beautiful and I fell in love with them. They had to catch a flight. I remonstrated with them, I even cried a little and they agreed to change their flight. I phoned a friend to come with us, because there were two of them", he said raising his eyebrows. "I made a picnic and we went by the lake, and in the evening we went out. They were drinking Calypso's, I was drinking lemonade. I went to the toilet and when I came back they had added alcohol to my drink. I was very angry, it made me sick. This was wrong", he said.

"What is this Bahar like?" he asked. He has spoken to her a couple of times a day to make arrangements. "She's lovely, I say. I was her supervisor for four years when she did her PhD in Nottingham. She's just finished and is with her parents in İzmir. My wife and I stayed with them last week." "How old is she?" Salman asks. "About thirty." "And she works?" "Yes she has started teaching architecture at the university in İzmir." "I think she could be good for me", he says with a knowing smile. "But you're married", I counter. "But my wife and I are not good these days." I say nothing. "She smokes. She can smoke but not in the house or when the children are home. She's always talking. She doesn't want me to be with tourists, with foreign women. But it's my job. She saw Bahar's name on my telephone. Who is this Bahar, she asked. And I left my Facebook open one day and she found a photo of one of my woman tourists who I loved and was very angry. I told her the truth – that I had been with this woman but wouldn't do it again. What can you do? The woman posted this photo of us both embracing. It's a dangerous thing, the Internet." I commiserate. "But her uncles would kill me if I tried to get a divorce. It was a mistake marrying her. I was young. I saw her at a friend's wedding, on the balcony and she looked beautiful. My father spoke to her family and I met her three or four times and we married. But now I regret it. She is Kurd. She's not educated. I need a woman like Bahar."

"Her father would kill you if the uncles didn't get you first", I promise him. But who am I to talk.

He shows me the main shopping street and we go in search of a car hire firm Bahar found on the Internet. We stop and I top up my Turkish phone. It's a Nokia like one of my old phones – maybe a few phones ago. It's fine,except friends of the old owner keep texting me. The car hire office is two floors up, past a hair salon on the first floor and people's washing drying on the landing. The office is seedy with old car catalogues on a coffee table and a surly unshaven man behind a desk. We talk about my leaving the car in Kars and he quotes an exorbitant sum for petrol and getting it back. So I say "OK two days and I'll bring it back here on Saturday night." "So you want the car", he says amazed. Sure, I say. "OK that's plus tax." Salman grins. I say fine and we shake.

Temporary camp, Van

Street life, Van

I ask if it's insured when we've left, as I'm suddenly hit by doubts. I can get a car at the airport for only 5 TL more. But its a tiny Hyundai. So Salman rings him and he says fully insured for crash. I ask Salman what would happen if I kill anyone on the road. He looks serious and says, "you will never finish paying. If you kill a child, the family would want blood money. They don't care about their children while they're alive, but if you hurt one you'll never hear the end of it."

In the hotel, later that night, I ask Scharlie to ring the Co-op Bank and check my travel insurance has personal liability. I give my details so she can access my account. The next morning I awake to a frantic email saying the bank threw a fit when she used my password and she's worried they may have blocked my account. I've worked out how to ring using the Skype, so I phone the bank. It's very early in the UK but they must have 24 hour service because they answer. The operator is a lively Liverpudlian – the Coop call centre is in Kirkby near Liverpool – who takes me through a load of security questions and resets my password. Luckily I'm allowed to keep the same pin and password and can use the same security questions. She has a record of Scharlie's call. She reads out the clause about personal liability and it sounds as if I'm covered. I certainly hope so. Then she wishes me a safe journey in Turkey.

Walking down one of the main shopping streets, Salman points out the hotel Urartu. "It used to be the best before the Rescate and Elite World", he says.

We have to call Bahar, so I suggest we sit in the lobby and I check out the hotel while he calls. I ask the price. The manager comes – a smiling baldheaded fat man with a wide smile and a gap between his front teeth. He seems delighted at the chance of showing off his hotel and takes me up to one of the rooms. Unfortunately carpenters are drilling the wall of the corridor to fix wooden decorative panels and it creates the wrong impression. He brushes it aside and waves me into the room. It's a bit overblown with a huge flat screen TV forming the bed end. He sees I'm impressed. I ask him how much and he says "I give you good price". It seems cheap. I'm paying more in the Rescate. I say I'll think about it. Back in the lobby he offers us tea. Salman is interested in all this. He's planning to open his own hotel; he believes the hotel business is a gold mine.

I asked the manager how he learnt English. He says he is interested in languages and he loves discovering new words. He throws out examples of words he's learnt recently. His vocabulary and diction are great for someone self-taught. I ask him if his children will go into hotel management. He says it's

Serap Kart, Hotel Elite World, Van

My room, Elite World

their decision but for him it's good – he likes relating to people.

Outside Salman says the best hotel in Van is now the Elite World built a couple of years ago. We have time and we're on a roll so I suggest we go and check it out. The reception staff call a manager to attend to us and a tall young woman arrives. She's from Ankara, it transpires from Salman's questions. She shows us around – one of the bedrooms, the conference facilities, the restaurant on the 10th floor, where she introduces me to the maitre de, the breakfast bar above the lobby, the bar where they have live music three nights a week and the place converts to a "Pub" after midnight, the patisserie on the ground floor and finally the highlight it seems, the fitness centre. We have to fit plastic covers over our shoes before we enter. She manages it deftly in her heels. There is a large tiled swimming pool. She relates its measurements – length 40m, depth 1-6m. She shows us the exercise room with its new machines, the steam bath, cold-water douche and sauna and then whisking open a door with a flourish, she reveals a naked man being lathered in soap by an Indonesian masseur. "Just for that it would be worth staying here", I quip as we head for the lift. Back in the lobby she asks us if we'd like tea. At first I refuse, saying we don't want to take more of her time but she looks disappointed, so I say yes. This tea ceremony is an important part of the etiquette here. She asked if we liked the hotel and if I'd like to stay here. I calculate it is about the same as in the Rescateand it will give me a chance to be in town the night before I had to collect the hire car. I say I'll take it. I ask how her English is so good and she say's she'd been studying in Bournemouth for a year. She liked England and had an English boyfriend who wanted to marry her, but she'd wanted to come back home and do something for her country. I ask her how she likes Van. She'd cried whn she first came to Van but had made friends. She'd had to sign a two-year contract when she took the job. She asks about my work and if Van was safe. I said the hotel looked safe. She grimaced and said how they had been told to stay in the hotel if there was another earthquake.

Thursday 27 September

Today is a day off. I'm not sure I've achieved much so far. But I have been on site and seen the place and got a feel for what's happening. So I'll know what people are talking about in Ankara and Istanbul. In a way it's about legitimising my findings.

Salman is taking me to see the Armenian Cathedral on Akdamar Island in Lake Van. It's a beautiful day and he's earlier than the 9 o'clock we agreed, which is fine. I quickly throw my water, sunglasses and guide in my pack and go down to the lobby and we set off with light heart. He accuses me of being quiet. I guess I'm digesting things. We pass people selling fish by the lakeside and Salman says he'll get some for his mother on the way back.

There is one solitary passenger waiting at the ferry – we need 16 to fill the boat but I'm feeling relaxed so I sit with him at the table while Salman gets out his computer and Internet dongle and goes to work. It turns out the other passenger is from Tallinn, Estonia. I say I've been there. We swap observations – too touristy and catering for Finns stocking up with fags and booze, we agree.

People arrive but not enough. Some leave. Salman asks me what I want to

Armenian Cathedral, Akdamar Island

Built by King Gagik 915-921

do as we've been waiting an hour and a half. I say we'll give it more time – we have nothing planned. I climb onto the new breakwater and observe the island and the church. It seems close enough to swim, especially since I've been told the lake is strongly alkali and has higher buoyancy than the sea. Finally two families arrive. Salman negotiates a discount. Despite this one of the passengers objects. His two children go free so it's just £2.50 more for him and his wife. He looks well off – new shoes, gold shades, telephone ear piece – maybe it's the principle.

Never mind, we set off across the blue lagoon to the fairy tale castle. We sit in the stern but as we get closer I go forward to take pictures. The guardian greets Salman. It's very informal and there doesn't seem anything to pay, or maybe I don't realise Salman is paying for me as I set off up the path exploring. I leave the regular path and climb through chapel ruins so I can see the cathedral from a distance. The red basalt stone is glowing in the morning light. It is beautifully compact – a neat cone rising to a conical roof. The walls are covered in relief carvings of scenes from the Bible as I walk closer I am delighted to decipher the stories – David and Goliath to the right of the main entrance, Adam and Eve, Daniel in the lions' den, and a delightful Jonah with a whale that looks like a pig.

In 300 AD Armenia was the first country to accept Christianity as a state religion. The Turks hadn't arrived and the whole of Anatolia was Armenian. I circumnavigate the church as other people begin to arrive and feel it's a pity I can't have it to myself a little longer. Inside I discover the walls are covered in biblical frescoes. There is a truly wonderful painting of Christ's head which looks

Relief carving of David and Goliath

Frescoe of Christ

Shade under almond tree

Medieval thomb stone

like a gentler version of the Turin Shroud. I wonder if it's genuine. So many of the people and places mentioned in the Bible are here in Turkey. Mary, mother of Jesus, is said to have lived at Ephesus. Other disciples were buried here and Paul developed most of the Christian message on his travels in his letters to the congregations he'd founded here.

Salman arrives and starts giving me his tourist guide patter, but he doesn't know the Bible and the guardian who's with him keeps correcting him. It's all in good humour; Salman is not really serious. We walk up through an almond grove. He says people eat them when they are green and sweet, as well as when they are ripe and you have to crack them open. There are none left of course. The trees have been stripped by picnicking Turkish families during the summer. Apparently this is a popular place to come and ferries shuttle back and forth all day. The Turks are not interested in the architecture or religious message, but in bar-b-ques and relaxing. We sit under the trees and chat. When a small English party comes up the path I salute them. A man says, "an Englishman! Where are you from?" "Cambridge". "Never heard of it", he jokes. He asks if I'm on my own. "Lucky man", he says. "They never stop talking", he says, pointing to the three women ahead. They are climbing the path that leads through a tunnel to the top of the hill. I'm not sure they'll make it. I'd like to try but it would take half an hour and we've arranged to meet back at the boat at 1 pm. Salman has disappeared, I assume back to the quay. So, rather reluctantly I turn back. I hop down the paved path and Salman says no need to rush as he was going to say I needed more time. He would have enjoyed keeping the other people waiting for his important English tourist. Nikita, the Estonian, has left his rucksack on board so I assume he's coming back and he turns up a minute later and we set off. From there being no one around, suddenly there are lots of people and boats. Maybe they come from another landing place or more likely we were just too early.

Salman has talked to Bahar who has said he should take me to see the new Toki houses on the hillside above the city, so we are heading back into town and I ask if it's all right to offer Nikita a lift. He's been hitching hiking across Turkey. He says the south, near Syria, is even drier than here and that the patches of green and occasional tree are an immense relief to someone from green Estonia. He's burnt from the sun and has a long untrimmed black beard. With his dark eyes he looks like an orthodox priest. He quizzes Salman about somewhere cheap to stay in Van. Salman gives him the name of a hostel and says he can stay at his uncle's hotel for only 10TL and have a room to himself. Nikita says the hostel sounds good. I ask him if he has been to England. "I have lots of friends who've been, but no I've only been to difficult places." He is an art historian. "I want to see them before they disappear", he says. "I'll go to England one day, when I'm old."

I ask Salman if there's anywhere else worth seeing – I can see a Toki development on my way back from Kars. "Hoşap Castle", he says. "But it's a long way." Nikita asks about it and if he can tag along. I look at Salman who looks a little peeved. "It's up to Stephen", he says. So I say, "sure you can come" and we set off, stopping to see a Seljuk cemetery. There is a chapel in some state of disrepair and wonderful tall slim basalt headstones with intricate carvings. One

Seljuk cemetery of Ahlat

Stele 12-13th Century

Hosap Castle

Children of Güzelsu

of the graves has recently been robbed. The stones are overturned and there is a big clean hole. I am shocked. Salman shrugs. "And you see why I insisted on going to the new hotel this morning and leaving my bag", I say. Salman grins. "It's not the same". He'd been reluctant to drive 10 km in the wrong direction to drop off my luggage before we set off this morning saying it would be perfectly safe in the minivan. I'd said OK if you have insurance or can indemnify me for any loss. Faced with responsibility he had laughingly given in. It is so much more relaxing without having to worry about luggage.

Hoşap is close to the Iranian frontier. We drive through countryside. Fields where the wheat and hay have been harvested. Mud brick houses with flat mud roofs. Stalks of hay: some dry, some green. And a two metre wall of dung like a dry stonewall in Derbyshire – wide at the base and tapering towards the top. Made by the women from round cowpats; fuel for winter. There are primitive looking sheep in the dry pasture, long haired with horns, more like goats than sheep. Stringy cattle grazing where there's water and it's still green. And all around this flat land, folded grey hills with suddenly flashes of red, orange and black where the rock is exposed. Nikita was right – this is an epic landscape. We pass a reservoir, half full now in autumn. There are striations on the red rocks and the land looks half formed. Where there is water it is green and there are more trees and rushes.

We see the castle high above to the left of the road. This was the silk road from the Orient and until recently, when the government clamped down, the village, like many others places, Van included, earned its living from contraband

View of Silk Road to Iran

Buying contraband petrol

petrol and cigarettes. Despite the clampdown there are still plenty of lorries and vehicles filling up from jerry-can-carrying salesmen outside the oily repair shops lining the roadside. We drive up the steep road to the castle entrance. It's been heavily restored, but is nevertheless most impressive in its simple grandeur. Salman says it is nearly time for prayers so he'll leave us to it. We climb the rocky passage leading from the outer gate to inner courtyard. Nikita asked if Salman is very religious. No just lazy, I say. And as we lean over the battlements to take in the view to the north we see him chatting to the various men hanging about. The gendarmerie is here today and we run into tough looking guys in civvies with Kalashnikovs. Apparently the Governor is coming later and this is the advance guard taking up position on the highest point of the castle. We explore as far as we are able and even advance beyond the tape saying no admittance but turn back when one of the armed police appears above us. We wave and exchange greetings. He wants to know where we are from. He is relaxed; we aren't going to get shot. Discretion dictates we go back. Salman introduces us to the Professor responsible for the restoration who is waiting to greet the Governor. Salman is telling him he needs a brochure and information for tourists. He has a website he says defensively.

We go back a different way over a high pass direct to Van. As everywhere in this border region, there are watchtowers on the high points, each within sight of the other. Nikita is interested in seeing an Armenian church near Van. Salman asks him if he wants dropping off. It would be an 8 km walk and it is 2 hours to dark, so he says he will go in the morning. We drop him in town and

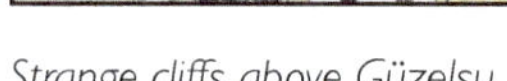
Strange cliffs above Güzelsu

Green amongst parched hills

point him in the direction of the centre and his hostel. We shake. I should take his contact details but I don't.

Salman drops me at my hotel. We walk down the road to a cash machine and I take out cash to pay him the rest of the money I owe him. I give him the crisp notes and he shakes my hand. Maybe he's used to having trouble with payment. I'll miss you business class, he says. I'll miss you too gigolo, I say. We hug and say goodbye. I've only been in my room a short while when he rings and he gives me new instructions about my route to Kars tomorrow. I should take the yellow road on my map – the red road is much longer. It is straightforward and I'm sure I won't get lost. I guess my six years in Venezuela has toughened me for potholed roads and bad drivers.

The hotel is very swish and my room is just as luxurious as Rescate. I shower, change and go to dinner. I called Serap, the young manager who showed me the hotel. She said she'd like to have dinner with me, but in the event has to work, but she meets me in the lobby and we have tea and she asks if she can have dinner with me on Saturday when I get back from Van.

The maître d' is on duty and recognises me. I am seated at a table in the middle of the room. I order lentil soup and fish – he recommends salmon – and a glass of white wine. The food is good and there is live music from two musicians, one on a twelve-string lute the other on a long thin recorder. Bahar rings and I tell her about my day and she says nice music. She has really been looking after me, ringing every day to see how I'm doing. I write the journal and then go to bed, Skype Scharlie and watch a bit more of a film.

Kars

Friday 28 September

My big day. I am up early, have breakfast at seven and am out looking for the car hire firm, which is up the road just after eight. I can't quite remember how far it was up the road, it seemed closer. I go into a shop with a Vodaphone sign and top up my phone for the trip. A young man, I think he's maybe the son of the man I saw on Wednesday, is on duty. He fills in the forms and I get him to talk with Bahar to confirm that the car is insured. He writes down her number. He passes it over for me to sign and I say I want to see the car first miming with my hands. He nods and we trot down to see the car. It is a silver Citroen C3, a bit battered, but will blend in. He shows me where the licence is kept behind the driver's sun visor and the spare wheel and tools in the boot. I get in, adjust my seat and mirror and I'm off.

I turn at the lights at the top of the road and head back down, past the hotel to join the main road north. I stop at a gas station on the corner and fill up. The petrol here is dearer than in the UK, in fact people have told me it is the dearest in the world. I am in a really good mood for driving – cautions, attentive but very confident. Always when embarking on something difficult – public speaking or perhaps a long climb in Scotland on my own, I do a quick biometric test. How am I mentally, physically, emotionally? Today I am good on all three. This is a red-letter day. I feel trepid but light-hearted. The sun is shining,

The road north to Kars

Haystacks for coming winter

the open road is ahead and I am on an adventure.

I know this first part of the road; we came this way to Erciş . The car is running fine. I have my map on the passenger seat and my phone, camera and water in the dashboard holder. Throughout the journey I constantly stop to take photos out of the window. So I keep overtaking the same lorries and slow moving vehicles. They must think I am mad. But the agriculture, the rock landscape, the hills and the people fascinate me and I want to record them. I reach the turnoff where I leave the known road and turn off north into the unknown.

Small hamlets, flat pasture, origami hills. The first town is Muradiye. It is confusing. There is a dual carriageway going through the town but the right hand carriageway is blocked with traffic – cars, vans and small trunks. I battle my way through. The road is dug up in places and I have to weave round piles of blocks and potholes. Then the road in front is blocked by a row of stones forming a wall and I realise that they are re-surfacing the right hand carriageway. So I turn and retrace my way and then dice oncoming traffic up the left hand carriageway. This happens in the next two towns I pass through. So as well as building the new highway they are also resurfacing the roads in the towns.

They would be easy but for the bad parking in town and the bad driving on the road. Although the highway is two lanes, plus a wide central reservation, everyone drives in the centre of the road. Even the big lorries and petrol tanks drive like this. Maybe they are accustomed to potholes or debris in the slow lane or maybe they are just crap drivers. So although the roads are like motorways (but without crash barriers, road markings or cats' eyes) you have to keep your wits about you.

As if poured like toffee onto the green pastures, there are great-heaped masses of jagged black rock. It is an immense lava field that has crystallised petrified into grotesque sinuous globs. It stretches as far as the eye can see up to a low rounded mountain. No wonder the land looks provisional and prehistoric.

I see big winged birds of prey that may be eagles. Young boys with sticks guard their flocks or stop the cows wandering into the road. We begin to climb towards the Tandurch Pass. A team of men are unloading galvanized steel by the side of the road. They are building a crash barrier. The first sign of a road safety measure I have seen and necessary because these bends are over a big drop. Near the top they are still digging out the mountain to widen

Petrified lava poured like toffee

Mount Ararat

the carriageway and the surface of the old road is pitted and broken. There is a cloud of dust from the vehicle in front, so I close my windows. I have been driving with the passenger window open since this car lost its air conditioning some time ago.

I cross the pass and see Ararat – cloud wreathed but with the summit snow covered cone peaking through. It is magnificent. Not the pudding I imagined but huge and magnificant, dominating the plain of Doğubayezit, the town that sits at its southern foot. I stop and take photos, trying to get some framing of the scene using the farmyard by the roadside. I stop a number of times as I get closer and the cloud dissipates. Entering Doğubeyazıt (Dogu) there is a sign to Ishak Paşa. The town is a mess to drive through, everyone trying to get through the crowded narrow streets. I realise I've gone wrong and turn round and pick up the right way. It's cobbled and rises out of the town to a red stone palace on a rock hanging at the head of the narrowing valley. It is spectacular and I am excited. There are curves up the final steep kilometre and then I am there and parking. There is nothing to pay and I wander in through the grand gated entrance into the main courtyard. To my right is the mosque and library and in front the entrance gate to the royal apartments and the 14 rooms of the king's harem. I go there first. There is a party of Germans which is a pain, but I am in a good mood and patiently wait until a room clears.

From a balcony in the harem I can look out over gorge to the crest of the ridge and up to the very head of the valley. Clinging to the sidewalls of the gorge there is a mud red castle with round towers and battlemented walls. It

Urartu castle

Ishak Paşa Palace, 1685-1784

looks precipitous. I wonder how the troops reached the walls and what they were defending. They are much older than the palace. They are from Urartu times while the palace is 18th century Ottoman.

I see the kitchens and haman or bathhouse, and the mosque, which is being renovated. There is a sign saying no entry which I ignore since I want to take a photo from its windows and stand under its marble columns. The Germans follow me. I go to the library and on leaving am distracted by someone's movement and don't bow enough and crack my head on the door lintel. Allah is telling me not to get above myself.

Back at the car I decide to walk up the stony track to get a photo looking back. A tubby German with a baseball cap races after me and overtakes me.

Library, Ishak Pasa

Audience Chamber, Ishak Pasha

Ishak Pasha Palace from hillside

The breche in Urartu castle wall

He climbs up to a high spot to photograph. I figure the road loops round. There is a family parked under a tree. They are cooking peppers on a tin bar-b-que a carpet to lounge on and a tea urn fired by wood. This is the favourite pastime in the summertime. As I imagined, the track curves round and I get a closer view of the castle. On the way down I see the same German puffing up the other side. The coach is loading up and the English contingent is already aboard. Some people are chatting in the square, so he'll need to hurry. It's so nice to be independent. I feel smug as I climb in the car and drive up to explore the head of the valley. I park outside the mosque in the road under a tree. There is a car park and teashop. All the visitors are Turkish, many under the trees on rugs with bar-b-ques.

Children are climbing a steep path leading to a breche in the cockscomb ridge. I can see the light shining through the narrow slot. I am full of energy and start up without a second's thought. There are two fathers with young sons ahead of me but I overtake them and arrive at the gap. My chest is too deep to fit unless I climb up a foot and squeeze through. I traverse along the narrow precipitous ledge and scramble down. I hear the little boy, behind in the gap say, look at the tourist.

I explore this way and that along the battlements and have to scramble down steps and traverse the rocks. As one might have imagined there is no other way down, unless I jump, so I go back. Two young Turks in their twenties have followed me and we climb back up to the breche together, me leading up the rock climb, made shiny by many feet. On the other side we shake. We are

Clambering through the breche

Scramlng round the ruined walls

Kurdish, they say proudly – not Turk! We walk back to the mosque. I bash the dust off my trousers, have a drink of warm water from my bottle, adjust my shades, and set off for Kars. Getting back through the town is straightforward and I find the highway north to Igdir.

I should be wised up but still get shunted into the right hand carriageway. But the way is blocked by two vans, so I reverse a metre and go through a gap in the central barrier into the left hand carriageway and dice with death again, followed by the cars behind me. The journey is accompanied by the constant presence of Mountain Ararat to the east until it is behind me and I enter a green, fruit growing area. There are stalls by the road selling apples, tomatoes, pomegranates, melons and plums. I am tempted to stop, but don't. I am very near the Armenian border and quite close to Anna's, our office manager's, hometown, – Yerevan. All this was once Armenia, long before it was Turkish. This land between East and West on the rich trade route, but sandwiched between rival neighbours – Persia, Byzantium, Babylonia has always been a dangerous place to settle. But here early Christianity flourished.

I am on the outskirts of Kars at last and feel my way through the town looking for the famous Hotel Kars. Kars means snow in Turkish – it can be up to 10 m deep here in winter. Orhan Pamuk's book Snow about women and headscarves is set here. It also boasts a collection of turn of the century Russian mansions. This town was in Georgia then. It is enjoyable exploring, driving gently up and down the streets. I follow a water tanker that is spraying the road, presumably to keep down the dust, and park at the top of the hill next to the governor's palace. I walk round the overgrown square with a statue that I first take to be Stalin and then realize is Ataturk in similar military garb. I still haven't found the hotel. So I ask for directions and learn I'm parked opposite – a most unprepossessing black basalt hump. I go in and enquire, but they are full. A party of weary English arrive in a mini bus. Perhaps they are people I saw earlier, perhaps not. They look lost.

My second choice is the Grand Hotel Ani, and I go in search. It is at the other side of the town and I ask directions from some schoolboys and again learn I am right there. The road in front of the hotel has just been re-laid with fresh tarmac and is closed. So I park and go and see if they have a room. I am intrigued by the lack of lights in the foyer and suspect there is a problem but can't be bothered looking elsewhere. I go up to the room, do my things and, while it is still light, set off to explore the town.

I walk most of the commercial centre getting my bearings and looking for somewhere to eat as I feel adventurous and don't want to eat in the hotel restaurant. Eventually, having dismissed numerous kebab places, I find a pide place (pide is Turkish Pizza) and ask if they can do one with cheese. Kars is also famous for its cheddar. The manager hesitates and then agrees. I see Ayran the yogurt drink in the fridge and ask for it. It is pretty good and does the job. I find my way back to the hotel without too much bother. Işin rings while I am walking. I tell her what I have seen today and she says she wishes she'd come. She explains that for the last couple of months she has been worrying about her relationship with Vojtech. "I am coming out of it, I will be all right", she says.

Russian mansions, Kars, 1878-1920

'Cheddar' cheese shop, Kars

Saturday 29 September

I worked on the Burnley paper last night and had to use earplugs because of the generator thumping away in the yard below. And then someone came in at four and banged around and woke me. Nevertheless I am at breakfast by seven.

I pay and ask directions out of town and am given a map. Unfortunately it already had a line marked on the photocopy which I mistake for the manager's directions and so turn the wrong way and get lost immediately. There is a black minibus sticking out into the road. There are people impatient behind me, so I squeeze through. But my wing mirror hits his van. In my mirror I see him – a swarthy unshaven dark haired Kurd – shouting and shaking his fist. I don't stop. He chases after me in his van and when the road widens at the bus station he roars past and throws his van across my path. I jink round him but he races past and blocks my path again. He leaps out and grabs my door handle to yank me out but it is locked. I raise the window. A crowd has gathered around the car – all shouting, perhaps fifty or hundred. I don't know what will happen. I hit his van but don't believe I caused any damage and he was parked a metre or more into the narrow road. He's remonstrating with the crowd and showing them the rear of his van and pointing to my wing mirror that is folded in. I nod and shrug. The crowd begin to smile. A man gestures that all will be well. A policeman arrives and the collective decision is he has no case. He throws up his hands and roars off. I open my door and get out and shake hands and, having righted my mirror, ask the way to Ani and set off again.

I finally find the ring road and a sign – 60km to Ani. This is a high plateau. There are wild horses and eagles on the telegraph poles. What must this land have been like on horse back or camel, before electricity, pylons and roads? I reach the village and can see, over the tops of the mud houses, the walls of the ancient city of Ani – rival to Constantinople, Cairo and Baghdad. Sacked by Tamerlane in 1200 AD and then hit by an earthquake in 14th Century and abandoned forever.

I am the first tourist to arrive and pass through the gate alone into the vast ruined city. All is rubble but for isolated structures – a gable wall, a tower and round base of a church, a cathedral, all spaced half a kilometre apart. It is already pleasantly warm in the hot sun and I set off in anti-clockwise direction, opposite to that suggested on the map on a signboard. I start at a Seljuk palace on the edge of the site. It has been too extensively renovated – the only building to have been so – but from here I can get the impression of the city as a whole.

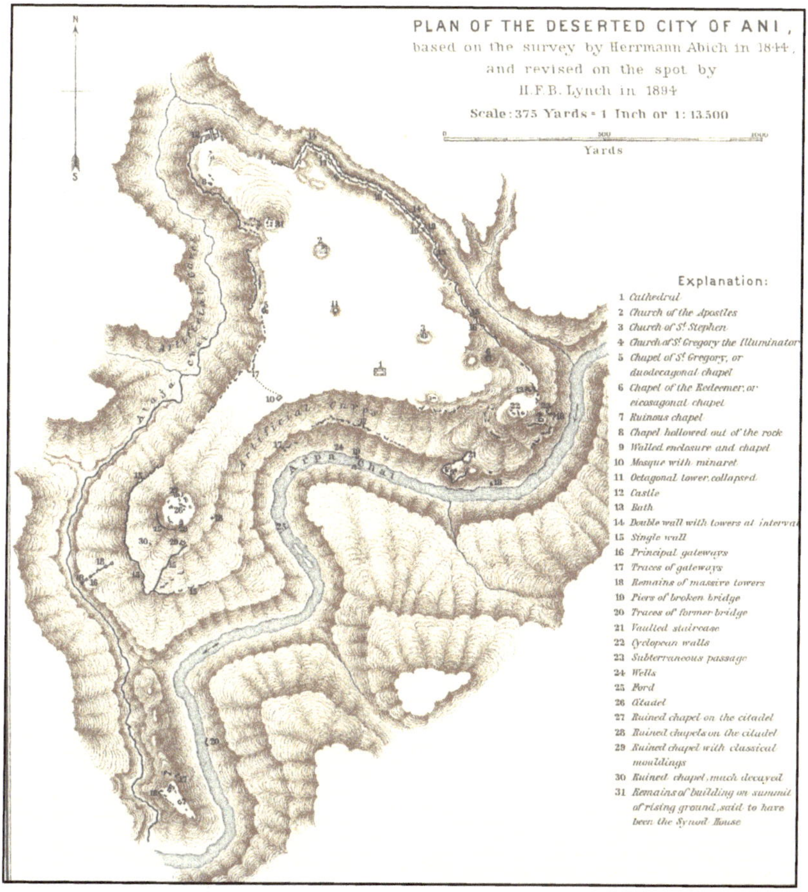

N
S

PLAN OF THE DESERTED CITY OF ANI,
based on the survey by Herrmann Abich in 1844,
and revised on the spot by
H.F.B. Lynch in 1894
Scale: 375 Yards = 1 Inch or 1: 13.500

Yards

Explanation:

1 Cathedral
2 Church of the Apostles
3 Church of S.t Stephen
4 Church of S.t Gregory the Illuminator
5 Chapel of S.t Gregory, or duodecagonal chapel
6 Chapel of the Redeemer, or eicosagonal chapel
7 Ruinous chapel
8 Chapel hollowed out of the rock
9 Walled enclosure and chapel
10 Mosque with minaret
11 Octagonal tower, collapsed
12 Castle
13 Bath
14 Double wall with towers at interva
15 Single wall
16 Principal gateways
17 Traces of gateways
18 Remains of massive towers
19 Piers of broken bridge
20 Traces of former bridge
21 Vaulted staircase
22 Cyclopean walls
23 Subterraneous passage
24 Wells
25 Ford
26 Citadel
27 Ruined chapel on the citadel
28 Ruined chapels on the citadel
29 Ruined chapel with classical mouldings
30 Ruined chapel, much decayed
31 Remains of building on summit of rising ground, said to have been the Synod House

Northern ramparts of Ani, 989–1020

Seljuk Palace main gate

St Gregory. (Polatoglu Kilesesi) 994

Mosque (Menüçehr Camii) 1072

The city is bounded to the east and west by rivers in deep gorges that meet at the southern end of the site in the bastion that is out of bounds. Young boys tend sheep in the green base of the western gorge. There are caves in the walls of the far side and ruined walls and watchtowers. I don't stay long and move on past a small twelve-sided church rather like Akdamar that is being renovated by a team of four masons. From there I cross the city and head for a tower. It turns out to be another church, now turned into a mosque. It is beautifully tranquil inside and through the stone windows I can see down into a deep gorge, with a river and trees that guard the eastern approach to the city. Again there are vestiges of wall and towers. Across the gorge new watchtowers atop slender legs rather than stone guard the modern border with Armenia.

Arpa Çayi river

Cathedral of Ani, 1010

Inside, the mosque is elegant with red and black stone in geometric patterns in the ceiling. There is a deep rectangular hole to the left of the entrance and I traverse delicately along a ledge to get a better view into the lower floors but it is too deep to climb out if I jumped down. I go back to the arched window over the ravine. Swallows are dancing in the rising air. I try and capture them on camera. One flies in and whistles round the ceiling vaults before disappearing. Outside the sign says it was built in the 11th century, one year after the Seljuk's defeated the Byzantines, and was the first mosque in Anatolia. There is a hand-made rustic ladder outside reaching to the parapet high over the main door. The minaret is very plain – an octagonal tower or chimney with just one panel of Arabic. While I am investigating the nearby remains of a row of houses the masons from the twelve-sided church turn up and start dismantling the ladder. It involves pulling away the legs till it crashes down and then hammering it apart.

I move on to the cathedral of Ani – a square red stone 10th century church with its roof intact apart from the done. There are no murals and it is quite plain, lofty and fine. Unfortunately others have arrived and I no longer have the place to myself. But it is a huge area, they are few and I am glad I am not here at the height of summer.

My next site is a beautiful church, only half of which is in fact still standing. A team of archaeologists are surveying it with theodolytes. It seems that the church was hit by lightning as recently as 1957 and has been supported by a massive steel skeleton. Next door is a haman and I am just thinking I have seen everything and can head back to the entrance when I see a couple descending

Church of the Redeemer, 1035

St Gregory's (Resimli Kilise) 1215

Double line of fortifications, 989

Sheep 'wolf' dog

into the ravine. I move to the edge and discover a beautiful Armenian church, also in red stone, with a squat steeple. It is a church of St. Gregory – the patron saint of Armenia. There are more people here. Clearly this is one of the high points of the tour. The church is built right on the edge of the ravine. This is river Araks or Akourian and is the border with Armenia and on the other side are abandoned Russian watchtowers. Inside the walls are completely covered in blue frescos depicting scenes from the life of St. Gregory.

I have seen enough, it is time to head back. But in the entrance gate I decide to walk the outside circuit of walls that guards the city to the north. I have been unable climb the citadel to the south because it is a military area and supposedly out of bounds. The soldiers are very nervous – a number have been killed only last week by PPK, the Kurdistan Worker's Party.

The outer walls are in a double row and I walk between the high inner wall and the low outer fighting wall.

I have a swig of my water and say farewell to Ani. I stop on the road back to photograph two sheep dogs. The first is black and as big as a wolf and lopes along parallel to the car. The second is black and white and is sitting watching the road. I stop and lower my window and raise my camera and it leaps at the car, its teeth snapping and growling loudly. I drop the camera, wack the car into gear and accelerate away. The dog just misses jumping through the window and grabbing me by the throat. I stop again to shoot an eagle on a telegraph post but it is leery and I do a u-turn to try again and catch it in flight.

The rest of the journey is less eventful. I realise I am not as sharp as

Mount Ararat

Toki housing, Van

yesterday so I drive carefully, seeing the same wonderful sights in reverse. I am particularly taken by a great-striated whaleback of the red stone.

I fill up in Tuzluca and stop again between Igdir and Doğubeyazıt, at a point I figure is closest to Mountain Ararat, to look for a way up. The mountain is completely clear today. When I first saw it this morning it was blurred by the dust in the air, but this close it is clear. I can see a village and dirt road climbing the mountain's flank. It is still a long walk from there. It can take 3-6 days depending on how much altitude sickness one is prepared to suffer.

Entering Van I stop at the Toki development near the main road and drive round the whole site taking photos. The apartments look much better than I expected and there are smart cars parked outside. Maybe poorer people got apartments on the hill 15 km away. There is a play park for children and lots of children playing out. It looks pretty good.

At the hotel I have a welcome shower and change. I am supposed to be having dinner with Serap but she texts to say her grandmother has died and she can't make it. So I dine alone again – this time on kebab. It is Saturday, there are a lot more diners and all of them smoking. So I beat a retreat to my room and work on my Burnley paper and finish it but for the illustrations and references.

Ankara

Sunday 30 September

I get up early and breakfast and start work on the paper. The deadline is tomorrow 1 October. And I want to publishwhat I learnt on my recent trip with Scharlie. But when I open the document, although the first page title is there, the rest is missing – 6,000 words have disappeared. I search for a backup but to no avail. I haven't done anything like this for years. How stupid. I don't have to leave for the airport till 1.30 and I can work on the plane. But is there time? It seems hopeless. I think of giving up. Pathetic. But I start anyway. I have all the original material – 18,000 words I chopped down. But all the new writing I have done over the last week and all the editing is gone. Nevertheless, I start in a methodical way, with the end rather than beginning, and get my discussion and conclusion written, when Bahar calls. I tell her my woes. She says it will be better the second time. I know she is right. It is fresh in your mind, she says.

I am making progress when, just after ten, Salman rings and says he's in the lobby as agreed and where am I. I go down and he invites me out for tea in the Street of the Scholars just up the road. I noted the other day how disgusted he'd been when I was charged 6 TRY for two teas in the hotel. We sit on stools and chat. He tells me a woman came and asked for his help yesterday. She had run away with her child and had asked if she could stay in his hotel. I asked why she had left her husband. "He had beaten her", he shrugged. "She is very beautiful." Are you going to help, I ask? "I can't. Her husband would kill me. The family would assume I'd slept with her. I told her to go back to her father and ask his forgiveness. But she won't and maybe some other man will abuse her."

I asked him how the house purchase in Istanbul was going. He said it was bought. How will you pay backthe money back in ten days? I ask. "I have to. It is my good name." Was it because one of your brothers wouldn't pay? "I can't say. But my friends help me. I can borrow from them. The family can be difficult." So what is your plan? "Long-term, to earn a living. I want to open a hotel, and do up the office so I have my own agency. I am going to make a company with the guide in Doğubeyazıt and another tour guide. We will be more powerful as three and we will not have to travel as much. And I will stop using the two agencies where I have to pay 20%."

I looked at your website and corrected the About us page, I tell him. "Yes thank you, that is good", he says. "Should it be in big letters?" No, not really, but I kept it in capitals because that's how you had it and I didn't correct some of it because I thought it was charmingly imperfect.

"My brother went with an uncle to Iraq, at the end of the war and they made a fortune buying nickel and titanium. They borrowed $2,000 from my father and bought one metric ton and drove it back here and sold it for $50,000. Now they have apartments in Istanbul and are rich. But my father didn't want me to go. He loves me and forbade me. But I don't want to be rich. I want to do good things."

What about the stock exchange? "I lost a lot when I had to sell quickly for the house. It is complicated, but I have my system now. I don't buy company stocks or petroleum any more, it is too difficult. I play the currency exchange market. I only want to recover what I lost and then I will stop. It is making me ill and I know it is not for me."

We walk back to the hotel and I go back to my article. I am making good progress but get a call from reception saying I should have checked out at twelve. I gather my stuff and, after paying, I settle down in the lobby and continue until a porter comes and tells me the shuttle is ready to go to the airport. They are half an hour early. I call Serap to say goodbye. She said she wanted to see me, but is still at breakfast. The shuttle is a smart black mini bus and drops me after a 10-minute journey. I tip the driver and go through security and get my boarding card. I have an hour and a half to take off so carry on editing. It is a tiny airport and virtually empty but half an hour later it suddenly fills as the bulk of passengers arrive.

Again I am in row 13 over the engines with a family with children next to me. I have discovered from the airlines website that this is the worst row and the only one that you can't pay extra for. A woman in a headscarf with lots of plastic bags and a small son sits next to me. I see the little boy wants to see out of the window, so we change places and I crash on with my paper. It is really rolling now.

All too soon we are landing in Ankara. There is no-one waiting so I sit in the café, get out my computer and find Tolga's number and ring. He is waiting in his car outside. Tolga is a young academic at METU, the top university here. He points out the 'squatter' settlements of beautiful detached homes surrounded

Tolga, calamari and turnip juice

Fish stall

by gardens and trees, that are being bulldozed to make way for apartments. Ankara is rolling over the countryside like a concrete blanket. Catapulting the place from subsistence farming to hi-tech living in the blink of an eye.

My hotel is in Kızılay, one of the nicest commercial districts with lots of eateries and shops. Tolga parks and waits while I drop my bags and we go in search of hamsi, local anchovies from the Black See, that are in season now. We cross a highway by a pedestrian bridge and reach an area of cafes and bars. He chooses a fast food fish bar attached to a fresh fish shop. We have to join a line waiting for a table and finally get a seat next to the road where we can watch the passers-by while we eat. Tolga orders calamari and turnip juice. I am hungry and it is marvellous. He walks me back to my hotel and I get to work on the paper and paste in my images and captions, read it through and send it off to the publishers. I can't quite believe I have done it. A 5000-word article with 10 illustrations in one day.

Monday 1 October

An email says the editors have received my paper and sent it off for review. Tolga collects me and we set off to Çankaya University to see Polat Gülkan, a top earthquake specialist and President of the International Engineering Association. Polat is delightful and very impressive. His English is impeccable and he's knowledgeable, erudite and to the point. He asks if we have time for lunch and our conversation ranges more widely over politics and Turkey and

Çankaya University

Tea house near my hotel

the future. He has just read Ian Morris 'Why the West Rules' and recommends it highly. He asks who else I am seeing and regrets I can't see Balamir.

After lunch we have time to kill before we see people at the Ministry of Environment, so he shows me his faculty of Architecture. The campus is huge and the photos on the walls from its founding show bare grassland. No wonder the trees on the hills are still small. The layout along a central axis and the design of the building is superb. He must have been a great architect.

Funda Torman. General Manager of the Urban Planning Department, sits at a big desk. She is relaxed and calm, but can't speak English. Her assistant, the chief planning officer in charge of the urban plan for Van thinks he can speak English but can't. At least I can't understand anything he says. They ask if I'd like to see the plans. There is a team of four young women pouring over a coloured plan of the city of Erciş and they are dealing with written objections. Both this and the plan for Van castle, are just land use plans showing the existing layout. There are no new projects, new road layouts or significant change of use – no real attempt to improve the urban design of the city. I am shocked and they can tell. They say it is too difficult, too political. Anyway, if they planned something radical the local authority would never implement it – so why bother.

Tolga drives back to the University and proposes we take a dolmu minibus into town so I can learn the system and come back on my own tomorrow morning, since we have an interview at nine and the traffic will be bad. He explains how to sit near the back and hand the fare to the person in front. It

METU, Department of Architecture

METU, Department of Architecture

is very easy and we are going from one terminus to, another so I can't fail. We say goodbye at Kızılay Square. I know my way back to my hotel from here.

I haven't gone that far when a well-dressed man approaches and introduces himself as Mithat, a chemistry teacher, and asks if I'd like to have tea with him. We walk a few hundred yards to a café with Turkish style cushioned bench seats and small stools. He orders tea and cakes. I am hungry and wolf mine down. He orders more tea. We chat about his family and life in Turkey. He says Ankara is a small city. He's taught himself English and would like to go to England one day. I decide to explore further and find a bar with a tree and sit at a table below its branches and order beer and watch the world go by. Later I find a bench in the street to listen to a zither player and I take a photo of two Green Peace volunteers chatting to a clown. The young man sends the woman across to speak to me. "Why are you taking a photo of us", she challenges. "Because you looked nice", I say. "You don't see to be having much success here." "No" she shrugs. A while later they take off their green waistcoats and go off arm in arm with two friends to a café.

Tuesday 2 October

More interviews today. Professor Nuray Karancı is a psychologist. She is knowledgeable and helpful – we talk about her work, trying to understand people's attitude to risk. I tell her about the lack of urban design. She tells me she studied in Liverpool and got mugged four times and then she lived in

Burçak Başbuğ

Anchovies

Hull. The implication being, she knows about British urban design. She is blond, about fifty, trim and elegant in a smart beige suit. She is sparkly and it is difficult to get a word in, but I do.

From here we walk through the campus to see Burçak Başbuğ who is in charge of the Disaster Research Centre. She studied at LSE and sent Robin and me her CV. She did her Masters in Warwick and says she loves England. She is helpful, especially in relation to the Turkish Insurance Pool and how they didn't stop selling policies after the first earthquake in Van. In the following two weeks lots of people bought insurance and they took a big hit when the second, more damaging quake hit a month later. She also talked about the Turkish Red Crescent and how they used 75,000 of their 90,000 tents in Van and how many people think this was crazy as most people want to live with their relatives in other places and villages in Anatolia.

We are heading for Eymir Lake when she rings and says she fixed for us to see people at AFAD, the Turkish relief and recovery agency that reports directly to the Prime Minister's office, so we turn round and go back. We interview four men, all geologists. The first two draw hazards maps at a province scale indicating the risk of landslides, earthquakes and avalanche. I ask about liquefaction and volcanoes. Not big risks in Turkey they say. The last two are responsible for choosing and then negotiating plots for Toki housing – some as many as 5,000 units or more. Given that Turkish families are typically as many as 10 or more, this is a big population. But they are geologists. Their main consideration is soil condition – which Polat Gülkan pooh-poohed as a major issue given that Toki housing is engineered with good foundations. They had nothing to say about life styles, culture, community building or any of the issues you might have thought would be important in such large new settlements. I ask who is responsible for creating a community. They either don't understand the question or have no answer. One says he has other people to see, he wants to get home. Tolga puts me on the Dolmu again. I am tired today, so before I walk back to the hotel, I sit in the dappled sun in the square for half an hour. That evening I find another fish restaurant and order anchovy in a bun and sit eating at a table before finding the same bar for a beer.

Wednesday 3 October

This morning Tolga comes for me about ten and we walk from the hotel to Gazi University to see Oktay Ergünay, another of the four gurus I've hoped to see. He is in his office with the younger head of their disaster unit, which is about to become an Institute.

Tolga kicks off as usual explaining my research in Turkish and asks if Professor Ergünay would like him to translate. He says yes, but then launches into pretty good English. He was in Toki and then Head of what became AFAD. He is very knowledgeable. He says he made many mistakes as a young man. We talk a lot about Toki housing and the tyranny of geologists' opinion being paramount. We also talk about repair rather than demolition. He relates how the authorities were horrified when he argued that a municipal building should

METU, Department of Architecture

METU, Department of Architecture

be repaired after the Erzurum earthquake in 1992. His young replacement gets bored and gets back to his office. He has probably heard it all before. But it is all new to me and useful. I scribble like mad. Finally we are finished, say goodbye and collect Tolga's ID at the gate.

Tolga says if I have nothing else to do would I like to have lunch with his family. I say sure. We drive towards his apartment, which is in the hills above METU. We discuss politics and the rise of Islamists in Turkey – supported since 2002 by the Erdoğan Government. There was an attempted military coup three years ago and many generals, Admirals and naval officers had been in jail for the past three years without charge. No one trusts lawyers or the legal system. And many journalists and others who criticized the government are also in jail. "So people keep quiet and don't criticize," Tolga says.

I meet his wife Melda, her mother and their new two month old baby Derin. Derin means deep or profound. We load up the car, the baby falls asleep and we drive to a natural lake in the hills called Eymir which is very popular at weekends with the diplomatic set that live nearby. It is unspoilt and the hills are covered in trees. This is part of the huge METU campus. I saw photos showing this area being terraced in 1940, but devoid of vegetation.

We find a restaurant and order fish and a plate of French fries, which Tolga loves. We have a couple of beers. Melda is a landscape designer, but hasn't actually made any gardens or done anything practical. She is studying sustainable settlements for her PhD and has another 18 months to finish. Tolga's time runs out in January and his head of department has freed him up

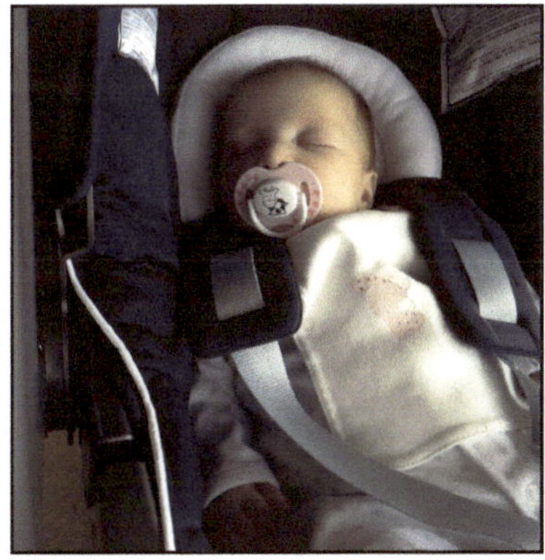

Baby Derin

Melda, Tolga's wife

this term to help him finish. I have agreed to read their synopses. Tolga says his supervisor is nice but knows as little as he does. Child development is her area and disasters are new to her. So they are learning together.

Tolga says that one of the big problems is that government keeps passing new laws. As well as being a problem for him with his PhD – he is studying the application of building codes and the training of inspectors – it is also a problem for the guys in AFAD. They said they were confused and didn't know what they were doing any more.

Tolga drops me at the dolmu again as they don't want to get stuck in a traffic jam in town. It is warm in the sun, the queue moves forward with each bus. After twenty minutes I get a seat, pay and fall asleep. I notice we have stopped moving and wake with a start. Some students giggle. .

At the hotel I sit on the terrace for a couple of hours writing till it gets cool then I collect my jacket and go off in search of pudding. I find a patisserie and order a milk pudding that has been cooked in an earthenware dish and two small rectangular baklavas of different kinds. I get a table outside and order fresh lemonade to go with the sweets. I stay an hour writing and wander back – dropping coins in the fiddler's case on the pedestrian bridge and in the palm of a woman in a shawl with an infant in her arms.

Istanbul

Thursday 4 October

I am dragged from deep sleep by the phone. My internal alarm usually wakes me before the alarm but not this time. I shower, shave, dress and pack quickly and methodically and I am just ready when Tolga telephones on the internal phone. I pay – it is good value – cheaper than the other hotels, but nice. The roads are clear as the lights are set to flashing orange. On the way to the airport Tolga tells me that the news has been full of reports from the border about the shooting of a Turkish village by the Syrian army. The military have called an emergency session of parliament to seek permission to enter Syria as this is the second provocation. They sent a warplane down a month ago and two pilots were killed. We talk at length about the Government positioning itself as the regional leader in the Middle East. At the last National Party

Crossing the Bosporus Bridge

Cihangir to Kabataş ferry

congress there were 200 delegates invited from neighbouring countries who were 'expected' to recognise Erdoğan's leading role in the region.

It is an easy journey, but further than I anticipated. I cannot thank him enough, yet it is he that says thank you. I say I will read his stuff. He says keep in touch. There is security at the entrance and then again into the departure lounge after checking in. They let me have two pieces of hand luggage.

I find a café near my gate and order çay which I have got used to it now and don't want filter coffee. I sit writing. I have a while to wait but it passes quickly and we board. There is a man asleep in my seat by the window, but I take the aisle seat and don't wake him. I nod off on the flight, which takes less than an hour.

The Havas bus to Taksim Square is waiting outside. It goes by the motorway which is much greener and wooded than my memory from last time. The Bosporus Bridge is spectacular and we climb a narrow twisting road through the old town to reach Taksim. From here I am pretty sure I will remember the way to the hotel.

My room is not ready, so I do my email in the lobby. I figure there is just time to catch the midday ferry to the islands Bahar has recommended. It is easy to find my way down the steep stone stairways of Cihangir. I reach the shore and walk to the ferry terminal and buy a bottle of water to get change to buy "jetton" or token for the ferry.

Having found a seat on the top deck near the prow I sit and watch the waves until we set sail. We pass the Queen Elizabeth cruise liner just entering

Ferry to the Princes' Islands

Holiday houses on Büyükada

the harbour. I recognise the Galata Tower, the Topkapı Palace and Blue Mosque. The journey takes an hour and the ferry stops at the three smaller islands before arriving at the last, Büyükada or 'big island'. I disembark with the remaining passengers and turn left by instinct along the promenade. The front is lined with fish restaurants. I am hungry and enter the most promising and ask for the table by the water. The waiter asks how many. I say one and he directs me to a table by the road. I understand but walk on ignoring his gestures of 'come'.

I try another with the same result. I have plenty of time and decide to continue walking. The crowds thin and the promenade opens to the sea and I have left the commercial centre. I am intrigued by the holiday homes, some

Fresh fish and salad

Sea front, Büyükada Island

of which are old timber mansions. After a couple of miles the path narrows behind the fish docks and I turn back and find a lovely restaurant with a garden, quite different from big tourist places, and order fish and salad from a tanned blond in a sundress. I stay a couple of hours and order Turkish coffee to finish. It is getting chilly and the table is in shadow, so I use the bathroom, pay and walk a hundred yards or so and find a bench in the sun and watch the boats go by and watch people swimming. This is a good time to come here. It must be unbearable in August with crowds and heat. Now it has an end of season feel of seaside towns of my youth. Eventually, I walk back along the main street to the clock where a road comes up from the ferry. I buy a jetton for the return trip, then an ice cream of walnut and chocolate and walk the other way along the top road. Lots of carriages pass – a strong smell of horse. There is a row of these carriages, the horses with their nosebags fixed, munching happily.

The houses here are real palaces – some are hotels, some look empty – perhaps closed for the season. I want to get back to the front and there is a steep staircase where the road turns inland. I stop for a while, sitting on part of the concrete breakwater, before going for the ferry. An Australian couple comment on two girls crawling past in Turkish trousers. I giggle, she notices and says they are not very flattering. People are boarding so I make a move and find a nice seat with a good view. I enjoy watching people board at each island. A middle-aged woman gets off at each landing stage and unloads a couple of plastic bags of fish. A dozen cats appear almost instantly. Then the gulls arrive, the cats chase them. The woman throws brown lumps, which I assume, are cat food. She is in a rush because only one or two passengers are still boarding

Bar off İstiklal Caddesi

View from Kandilli

and the ferry will go without her. I nod off for a minute and wake with a start. It is dusk as we approach the Golden Horn and the Sultanemet Mosque and Topkapı are illuminated with coloured fairy lights. The Queen Elizabeth, now at her berth below Beyoğlu, is also brightly light as is the Galata Bridge and Tower.

Can, pronounced Jan, from the Kandilli Observatory, has rung and invited me to a drink tonight and tomorrow I will meet his colleagues and might have to give a presentation to his students in the afternoon. He rings from the lobby. We turn left and walk up to İstikal Avenue, the famous pedestrian street of İstanbul that runs from Taksim down to Galata. There is a protest march against the war with Syria and Can says war is not likely. We enter a side street crowded with pavement bars and patrons on stools at small tables. There is a noise of many conversations, the bubbling hive of movement. Patrons greet Can but we move on because there are no seats on the pavement. Can is divorced – he sees his little boy who is four at the weekends – and he probably spends a lot of time here with his friends as he lives nearby.

We find a place and order beer. Can tells me about his work at Kandilli – the rapid response mapping, that produces estimates of damage and casualties and the early warning system that gives two seconds warning of a big earthquake, sufficient time to shut down critical things, like the gas supply to the city which would start fires. I have a second beer and we wander back to the hotel, read my emails, Skype and watch a film.

Friday 5 October

Can is collecting me in the car at ten and wants me waiting by the kerb as there is nowhere to stop outside the hotel. I had got up early to modify the Power Point to give his students this afternoon. I have added three slides about Turkey.

On the drive to the Observatory, which is across the Bosporus on the Anatolian side, we talk about Istanbul. It has 17 million and still growing. The effect of the second bridge higher up encouraged the city to expand dramatically. He points out a squatter settlement. He was working here on the bridge as a young engineering student 15 years ago and watched people rebuild their houses each night after the authorities had demolished them the previous day. They are building a mosque. There is a fundraising sign. "They think that if they have a mosque, the municipality will not push them out", he says. He points to the other sides of the road where homes have been cleared and the slope terraced and landscaped next to the motorway, but the mosque has been left.

Kandilli is on the top of a hill overlooking the Bosporus with a great view. There are separate buildings dating from the seventies or eighties and a small astronomical domed observatory dating from the mid 19th century, which gives the place its name. The buildings house the Meteorological Observatory and the National Earthquake Warning Station as well as the University earthquake observatory and other units I can't remember. He shows me round and introduces me to his colleague Cüneyt, pronounced "June eight". There is going to be a meeting, but first he shows me the systems he told me about last night and the screens that are monitoring 100 sensors on structures across the city for the rapid response mapping and the 10 sensors in and around the Marmara Sea that produce the early warning.

We go into the conference room and I am introduced to two others – Bilgen a member of staff interested in the social aspects of recovery and Özge, an MSE student. Bilgen says she can't stay, but in fact does. They ask about my trip and ask for my presentation. I say I can tell them about Chile and New Zealand, but it is early days to say much about Turkey.

The presentation goes down well. They interrupt quite a bit and there is a good discussion about how my findings relate to Turkey. They agree with my list of issues and like the paradox about Islam and the Turkish mentality. I say many people said the disaster in Van was an act of God – a punishment for bad ways. They are fatalistic about disaster and death, but the Turkish also love gambling, which is forbidden in the Koran. They love dicing with death. When the Turkish Insurance Pool continued selling policies after the first quake, lots of people bought insurance. But not like we buy insurance in England as a long-term commitment. They bought it like a lottery ticket with 50/50 chance of a payout. They laughed and agreed.

Özge, the student, gives a presentation about the work of the Red Crescent in Van. I assume it is her own research work and quiz her about the wisdom of using so many tents, but then realise she has been asked to translate the reports specially for my visit and I am touched by all the work it must have been.

We drive five minutes to a new restaurant, where Can and Cüneyt are taking me to lunch, and sit on the roof terrace with a view of the sea. They point out the main campus across the Bosporus in a wooded area overlooking the water. Can's friend is getting married in a place near the Syrian border and they are both going. We joke that they will be in a war zone. It is not like you see on TV says Can. But there has been another shooting by Syria and nobody knows if it is really a mistake and what will happen.

We go back to the department and we both work on the Power Points we will give his students this afternoon. I am adding slides about the masonry building in Christchurch because people were interested this morning. Bilgen was especially shocked that New Zeeland was destroying its heritage. She is big on cultural identity and I agree with her but realise that passionate outrage can be overwhelming and decide to tone down my delivery to the students.

We are cutting it fine, but Can knows all the back streets and we park with 10 minutes to spare and go in search of a lecture room. Just like Nottingham, it is a stressful muddle at the beginning of term. This is the first, introductory lecture.

Can is nice – tells them about the course and introduces the topic. He says that there will be a big earthquake around Istanbul every 100 years – but the students feign boredom. Then I am on. I drag a chair over so I can sit and set up. It goes well. They come up at the end to ask questions. They want to know what I think of Istanbul. I say it looks great after Van. But It is out of control, they say and look depressed. "Turkey is booming and the important thing, since you graduate next year is that you will get jobs", I say. But meanwhile the city is going to pot and the traffic is impossible, they say.

Earthquake early warning stations

Bogaziçi University

Can has to check on his room for Monday, so we climb some steps to the main administrative building. While he is there I climb to the large grass quad and realise that this is Boğaziçi University where I came before to give a paper with Bahar. It is sunny and lots of students are sitting on the grass. Can says that it used to be an American College for boys.

There is a lot of traffic. It is about five, so we have tea and sit on a wall overlooking the Bosporus because the café is full of students. Can spent six years in Japan and speaks good Japanese – I heard him talking on the phone arranging a visit of some Japanese to the Health Ministry. Japanese and Turkish are close. The sentence structure is similar and Can found it easy to learn – he just needed the vocabulary.

He says one of the big differences is that the campus is empty in Japanese Universities – students come to lectures then go to the library or home to work, or have a part time job. Here students hang out in cafes in preference to all types of work, including going to lectures.

It is still crowded when we leave the university but once round the jammed roundabout Can takes a narrow road through areas of expensive mansions straight down to the coast road. We drive to Ortaköy. There are restaurants and we decide to stop here rather than struggle to Taksim. We find a back street parking where the young attendant's job is to juggle cars as people come and go.

We walk down to the square in front of the ferry where there are restaurants. A shoe-shine man points to my shoes and I say no at first, then

Can getting his shoes shined

Fish restaurant, Ortaköy

agree. There is a circular bench under a plane tree and we can watch the world go by. It is Friday evening, people are in weekend mode and he makes my shoes look like new and then goes to work on Can's.

We find a fish restaurant and Can orders bream with a glass of white wine and a salad. We talk about Armenia. Can says his family came from near Van and were part Armenian and he can trace his ancestry back to the 11th Century. His great grandfather sheltered Turkish troops going north to fight the Russians when they were caught by winter snow. He was awarded 14 villages for his patriotism. "My father says we can't very well go and claim our land now", he says. He does not accept there was genocide and believes that there were atrocities by all sides – it was wartime, and if some died most left to go abroad.

On the Kurdish question he says Erdoğan was in talks with Kurdish leaders, but the opposition found out and demanded to know what was discussed. Erdoğan said nothing had been agreed. "When we know more we will let the public know" he said. We talk about Northern Ireland and Thatcher's role in starting secret talks.

We walk around the Mosque which is being renovated but there are still calls to prayers. He says that the Iman used to climb the minaret but now he uses a loudspeaker. There must be lots of fat clerics, I say. He asks if they call to prayer in England. I say we may be a tolerant nation, but I don't think we would suffer this racket in the mosque round the corner in Cambridge. He shows me the bridge covered in blue fairy lights. There are lots of young people taking photos and a row of stalls all selling the same baked potato, or kumpir, with a variety of fillings.

Bogaziçi Bridge

Inntal Valley, Austria

We drive back past the Ottoman summer palaces, past the football stadium, climbing the crowded avenue to Taksim. Someone is unloading drinks just before my hotel. So I jump out, get my bag from the boot, shake his hand warmly and reach my hotel.

Saturday 6 October

I wake naturally at 6 can make the 7 o'clock shuttle which says it takes 1.5 hours depending on traffic. I get a seat at the front; we leave on time and it takes half an hour so I am at the airport two hours early. Is this a record? It is all a breeze – the security check, a second security line and passport control. I find a café and order croissant and espresso macchiato – I am already back in Cambridge café mode. I spend a quiet couple of hours writing and board the plane – in Row 3, amazing. I have nearly finished this journal. Now waiting for take-off. What a trip! I am a seasoned traveller after all these years of nervous journeys. It has gone well. I have what I need to begin my report. I have made new friends and understood something of another country.

Two young American girls croaking like baby crows are in the seat behind me. I am so wanting to be home. We are 15 minutes late taking off – a passenger has stomach pain and got off. We take off and cross the Dardanelles. I can just glimpse the Golden Horn and the Blue Mosque through the clouds. Then we follow the Black Sea Coast north – a long line of sandy beaches and blue sea.

We follow the Danube through Romania, Bulgaria, and Austria. There is snow on the Alps. I can see Innsbruck and the Brenner Pass into Italy. Over the channel there are wind turbines in the shoals and the Thames looks majestic. The woman next to me had fidgeted the whole journey, the man in front had snored, the child over the aisle had shrieked. But the sun is shining and I am really home.

www.ingramcontent.com/pod-product-compliance
Lightning Source LLC
LaVergne TN
LVHW052257100826
845147LV00001B/72